TO

Elizabeth

FROM

Aevana

DATE

June/12 2010

VeggieTales®

30 VERY VEGGIE DEVOS ABOUT PATIENCE

Scripture quotations are taken from:

The Holy Bible, King James Version

The Holy Bible, New International Version (NIV) Copyright © 1973, 1978, 1984, by International Bible Society. Used by permission of Zondervan Publishing House. All rights reserved.

The Holy Bible, New King James Version (NKJV) Copyright © 1982 by Thomas Nelson, Inc. Used by permission.

The New American Standard Bible®, (NASB) Copyright © 1960, 1962, 1963, 1968, 1971, 1972, 1973, 1975, 1977, 1995 by The Lockman Foundation. Used by permission.

Holy Bible, New Living Translation, (NLT)copyright © 1996. Used by permission of Tyndale House Publishers, Inc., Wheaton, Illinois 60189. All rights reserved.

The Message (MSG)- This edition issued by contractual arrangement with NavPress, a division of The Navigators, U.S.A. Originally published by NavPress in English as THE MESSAGE: The Bible in Contemporary Language copyright 2002-2003 by Eugene Peterson. All rights reserved.

New Century Version®. (NCV) Copyright   © 1987, 1988, 1991 by Word Publishing, a division of Thomas Nelson, Inc. All rights reserved. Used by permission.

The Holman Christian Standard Bible™ (HCSB) Copyright © 1999, 2000, 2001 by Holman Bible Publishers. Used by permission.

International Children's Bible®, New Century Version®. (ICB) Copyright © 1986, 1988, 1999 by Tommy Nelson™, a division of Thomas Nelson, Inc. All rights reserved. Used by permission.

Cover Design by Big Idea Design
Page Layout by Bart Dawson

ISBN 978-160587-130-1

Printed in the United States of America

VeggieTales®

30 VERY VEGGIE DEVOS ABOUT PATIENCE

TABLE OF CONTENTS

A Message for Parents   9

A Message for Kids   11

1. Patience Is   15

2. When I'm Angry   19

3. Listening to God   23

4. Waiting for Your Turn   27

5. The Golden Rule and Patience   31

6. There's a Time for Everything   35

7. Praying for Patience   39

8. Being Patient with Brothers, Sisters,

                    and Cousins   43

9. How Patient Would Jesus Be?   47

10. If at First You Don't Succeed   51

11. Think First, Speak Later   55

12. When You're in a Hurry   59

13. More Patient Every Day   63

14. When Things Go Wrong   67

15. Speaking the Right Words at
    the Right Time   71

16. It's Up to You   75

17. Patience at Home   79

18. Words Are Important   83

19. It Starts on the Inside   87

20. Being Patient with Parents   91

21. Peace Is Wonderful   95

22. Being a Patient Friend   99

23. What the Bible Says   103

24. It's Better to Be Patient   107

25. Always Growing Up   111

26. Being Patient with Everybody   115

27. Stop and Think   119

28. Avoiding Quarrels   123

29. If You Need Help, Ask God!   127

30. With Love in Your Heart   131

Bible Verses to Memorize   135

A MESSAGE FOR PARENTS

If you're already familiar with VeggieTales®, you know the importance of providing your youngster with a steady stream of big ideas from God's Word. And this VeggieTales® devotional book can help you do just that.

This little text contains 30 brief chapters, one for each day of the month. Each chapter consists of a Bible verse, a brief story or lesson, kid-friendly quotations from notable Christian thinkers, a timely tip, and a prayer. Every chapter examines a different aspect of an important Biblical theme: patience.

So please try this experiment: For the next 30 days, take the time to read one chapter each night to your child, and then spend a few moments talking about the chapter's meaning. By the end of the month, you will have had 30 different opportunities to share God's wisdom with your son or daughter, and that's good . . . very good.

If you have been touched by God's love and His grace, then you know the joy that He has brought into your own life. Now it's your turn to share His message with the boy or girl whom He has entrusted to your care. Happy reading! And may God richly bless you and your family now and forever.

A MESSAGE FOR KIDS

Have you seen the VeggieTales® episode called *Abe and the Amazing Promise?* If so, you learned about the story of Abraham and Sarah, a husband and wife who waited, and waited and waited some more for a promised child. And, you may also remember how Bob the Tomato and his merry crew of Veggie-film-makers were delayed time and again by a series of hilarious filming disasters. So what did everybody in that episode need? They all needed patience, and so do you! That's why the big ideas in this book—ideas about what it means to be a more patient person—are really important.

So for the next month, ask your mom or dad to help you read a chapter a day. When you do, you'll soon figure out that that patience pays . . . in more ways than one.

Always be humble and gentle.
Be patient
and accept each other
with love.

Ephesians 4:2 ICB

DAY 1

PATIENCE IS

Always be humble and gentle.
Be patient and accept each other with love.
Ephesians 4:2 ICB

The dictionary defines the word "patience" as "the ability to be calm, tolerant, and understanding." Here's what that means: the word "calm" means being in control of your emotions (not letting your emotions control you). The word "tolerant" means being kind and considerate to people who are different from you. And, the word "understanding" means being able to put yourself in another person's shoes.

If you can be calm, tolerant, and understanding, you will be the kind of person whose good deeds are a blessing to your family and friends. They will appreciate your good deeds, and so will God.

No matter what we are going through,
no matter how long the waiting for answers,
of one thing we may be sure. God is faithful.
He keeps His promises. What He starts,
He finishes...including His perfect work in us.

Gloria Gaither

Be patient. God is using today's difficulties
to strengthen you for tomorrow.
He is equipping you. The God who makes
things grow will help you bear fruit.

Max Lucado

TODAY'S BRIGHT IDEA

Since you want other people to be patient
with you, you should be patient with them,
too.

PRAYER OF THE DAY

Dear Lord, sometimes it's hard to be
a patient person, and that's exactly
when I should try my hardest to
be patient. Help me to follow
Your commandments by being
a patient, loving Christian,
even when it's hard.
Amen

DAY 2

WHEN I'M ANGRY

A person who does not quickly get
angry shows that he has understanding.
But a person who quickly loses his temper
shows his foolishness.

Proverbs 14:29 ICB

When you're angry, you will be tempted to say things and do things that you'll regret later. But don't do them! Instead of doing things in a hurry, slow down long enough to calm yourself down.

Jesus does not intend that you strike out against other people, and He doesn't intend that your heart be troubled by anger. Your heart should instead be filled with love, just like Jesus' heart was . . . and is!

Take no action in a furious passion.
It's putting to sea in a storm.

Thomas Fuller

When you strike out in anger,
you may miss the other person,
but you will always hit yourself.

Jim Gallery

TODAY'S BRIGHT IDEA

Time out! If you become angry, the time to
step away from the situation is before you say
unkind words or do unkind things—not after.
It's perfectly okay to place yourself in "time
out" until you can calm down.

PRAYER OF THE DAY

Dear Lord, help me not to be
an angry person, but instead, make me
a forgiving person. Fill my heart
not with anger, but with love
for others . . . and for You.
Amen

DAY 3

LISTENING TO GOD

The thing you should want most is
God's kingdom and doing what God wants.
Then all these other things you
need will be given to you.

Matthew 6:33 ICB

God has a perfect idea of the kind of people He wants us to become. And for starters, He wants us to be loving, kind, and patient—not rude or mean!

The Bible tells us that God is love and that if we wish to know Him, we must have love in our hearts. Sometimes, of course, when we're tired, angry, or frustrated, it is very hard for us to be loving. Thankfully, anger and frustration are feelings that come and go, but God's love lasts forever.

If you'd like to become a more patient person, talk to God in prayer, listen to what He says, and share His love with your family and friends. God is always listening, and He's ready to talk to you . . . now!

In the soul-searching of our lives, we are to
stay quiet so we can hear Him say all that
He wants to say to us in our hearts.

Charles Swindoll

In prayer, the ear is of first importance.
It is of equal importance with the tongue,
but the ear must be named first.
We must listen to God.

S. D. Gordon

TODAY'S BRIGHT IDEA

Quiet please! This world is LOUD! To hear
what God has to say, you'll need to turn down
the music and turn off the television long
enough for God to get His message through.

PRAYER OF THE DAY

Dear Lord, help me remember
the importance of prayer.
You always hear my prayers, God;
let me always pray them!
Amen

DAY 4

WAITING FOR
YOUR TURN

Let everyone see that you are
considerate in all you do.

Philippians 4:5 NLT

When we're standing in line or waiting for our turn, it's tempting to scream, "Me first!" It's tempting, but it's the wrong thing to do! The Bible tells us that we shouldn't push ahead of other people; instead, we should do the right thing—and the polite thing—by saying, "You first!"

Sometimes, waiting your turn can be hard, especially if you're excited or in a hurry. But even then, waiting patiently is the right thing to do. Why? Because parents say so, teachers say so, and, most importantly, God says so!

It's not difficult to make an impact on
your world. All you really have to do is
put the needs of others ahead of your own.
You can make a difference with
a little time and a big heart.

James Dobson

What is your focus today?
Joy comes when it is Jesus first,
others second...then you.

Kay Arthur

TODAY'S BRIGHT IDEA

The next time you're standing in line, don't try
to push ahead of your neighbors. After all, if
you don't want other people breaking in front
of you, then you shouldn't break in front of
them!

PRAYER OF THE DAY

Dear Lord, let me be a courteous
person. Let me treat other people
with patience and respect.
And, let the things that I say
and do show my family and friends
that I love them . . . and You.
Amen

THE GOLDEN RULE AND PATIENCE

Do for other people the same things you
want them to do for you.

Matthew 7:12 ICB

Jesus gave us a Golden Rule for living: He said that we should treat other people in the same way that we want to be treated. And because we want other people to be patient with us, we, in turn, must be patient with them.

Being patient with other people means treating them with kindness, respect, and understanding. It means waiting our turn when we're standing in line and forgiving our friends when they've done something we don't like. Sometimes, it's hard to be patient, but we've got to do our best. And when we do, we're following the Golden Rule—God's rule for how to treat others—and everybody wins!

Seek to do good, and you will find that
happiness will run after you.

James Freeman Clarke

Be enthusiastic. Every occasion is
an opportunity to do good.

Russell Conwell

TODAY'S BRIGHT IDEA

What's good for you is good for them, too: If
you want others to be patient with you, then
you should treat them in the same way. That's
the Golden Rule and it should be your rule,
too!

PRAYER OF THE DAY

Dear Lord, make me a patient
person and let me be a person
who observes the Golden Rule.
Let me be understanding and kind,
and let me be quick to forgive others,
just as You have forgiven me.
Amen

THERE'S A TIME FOR EVERYTHING

There is a time for everything, and a season
for every activity under heaven.

Ecclesiastes 3:1 NIV

We human beings can be so impatient. We know what we want, and we know exactly when we want it: RIGHT NOW! But, God knows better. He has created a world that unfolds according to His own timetable, not ours.

As Christians, we must be patient as we wait for God to show us the wonderful plans that He has in store for us. And while we're waiting for God to make His plans clear, let's keep praying and keep giving thanks to the One who has given us more blessings than we can count.

The God who gives the flowers their
beauty and the birds their daily food
also gives His people all that they need,
just when they need it.

Warren Wiersbe

Your times are in His hands. He's in charge of
the timetable, so wait patiently.

Kay Arthur

TODAY'S BRIGHT IDEA

Big, bigger, and very big plans. God has very
big plans in store for your life, so trust Him
and wait patiently for those plans to unfold.
And remember: God's timing is best.

PRAYER OF THE DAY

Dear Lord, sometimes I become
impatient for things to happen.
Sometimes, I want the world to unfold
according to my plan, not Yours.
Help me to remember, Lord,
that Your plan is best for me, not just
for today, but for all eternity.
Amen

PRAYING FOR PATIENCE

Do not worry about anything. But pray
and ask God for everything you need.

Philippians 4:6 ICB

Would you like to become a more patient person? Pray about it. Is there a person you don't like? Pray for a forgiving heart. Do you lose your temper more than you should? Ask God for help.

Whatever you need, ask God to help you. And, as you pray more, you'll discover that God is always near and that He's always ready to hear from you. So don't worry about things; pray about them. God is waiting . . . and listening!

God insists that we ask, not because
He needs to know our situation, but because
we need the spiritual discipline of asking.

Catherine Marshall

So often we pray and then fret anxiously,
waiting for God to hurry up and do
something. All the while God is waiting
for us to calm down, so He can do
something through us.

Corrie ten Boom

TODAY'S BRIGHT IDEA

Pray early and often: One way to make sure
that your heart is in tune with God is to pray
often. The more you talk to God, the more
He will talk to you.

PRAYER OF THE DAY

Dear Lord, You are always near;
let me talk with You often.
When I am impatient, let me turn
to You. And, let me use prayer
to find the peace that You desire
for my life today and every day.
Amen

BEING PATIENT WITH BROTHERS, SISTERS, AND COUSINS

Show respect for all people. Love the
brothers and sisters of God's family.

1 Peter 2:17 ICB

How easy is it to become angry with our brothers, sisters, and cousins? Sometimes, very easy! It's silly, but it's true: sometimes we can become angry with the very people we love the most.

The Bible tells us to be patient with everybody, and that most certainly includes brothers and sisters (if we're lucky enough to have them). We must also be patient and kind to our cousins and friends. Why? Because it's the right thing to do, and because it's God's commandment. Enough said!

Weak things united become strong.

Thomas Fuller

It never ceases to amaze me the way
the Lord creates a bond among believers
which reaches across continents,
beyond race and color.

Corrie ten Boom

TODAY'S BRIGHT IDEA

Say it! If you love your brother or sister (and,
of course, you do!) say so. But don't stop
there: let all your family members know that
you love them . . . a lot!

PRAYER OF THE DAY

Dear Lord, let me be respectful
of all people, starting with my family
and friends. And, let me share
the love that I feel in my heart
with them . . . and with You!
Amen

HOW PATIENT WOULD JESUS BE?

Let me give you a new command:
Love one another. In the same way
I loved you, you love one another.

John 13:34 MSG

If you've lost patience with someone, or if you're angry, take a deep breath and then ask yourself a simple question: "How would Jesus behave if He were here?" The answer to that question will tell you what to do.

Jesus was quick to speak kind words, and He was quick to forgive others. We must do our best to be like Him. When we do, we will be patient, loving, understanding, and kind.

God gave everyone patience—
wise people use it.

Quips, Anonymous

Patience is the companion of wisdom.

St. Augustine

TODAY'S BRIGHT IDEA

When in doubt: do the thing that you think
Jesus would do. And, of course, don't do
something if you think that He wouldn't do it.

PRAYER OF THE DAY

Dear Lord, let me use Jesus as
my example for living. When I have
questions about what to do or how
to act, let me behave as He behaved.
When I do so, I will be patient, loving,
and kind, not just today, but every day.
Amen

DAY 10

IF AT FIRST YOU DON'T SUCCEED

But the people who trust in the Lord
will become strong again. They will
rise up as an eagle in the sky.
They will run without needing rest.
They will walk without becoming tired.

Isaiah 40:31 ICB

Perhaps you've tried to become a more patient person, but you're still falling back into your old habits. If so, don't be discouraged. Instead, be even more determined to become the person God wants you to be.

If you trust God, and if you keep asking Him to help you change bad habits, He will help you make yourself into a new person. So, if at first you don't succeed, keep praying. God is listening, and He's ready to help you become a better person if you ask Him...so ask Him!

We are all on our way somewhere.
We'll get there if we just keep going.

Barbara Johnson

Your life is not a boring stretch of highway.
It's a straight line to heaven. And just look
at the fields ripening along the way.
Look at the tenacity and endurance. Look at
the grains of righteousness. You'll have quite
a crop at harvest...so don't give up!

Joni Eareckson Tada

TODAY'S BRIGHT IDEA

Forgive . . . and then forgive some more!
Sometimes, you may forgive someone once
and then, at a later time, you may become
angry at that very same person again. If so,
you must forgive that person again . . . and
again . . . until your forgiveness is complete.

PRAYER OF THE DAY

Dear Lord, help me to become
a person whose habits are pleasing
to You. Help me to change
my bad habits so that nothing can
interfere with my love for others
or with my love for You.
Amen

DAY 11

THINK FIRST, SPEAK LATER

The wise accumulate knowledge—
a true treasure; know-it-alls
talk too much—a sheer waste.

Proverbs 10:14 MSG

When we become frustrated or tired, it's easier to speak first and think second. But that's not the best way to talk to people. The Bible tells us that "a good person's words will help many others." But if our words are to be helpful, we must put some thought into them.

The next time you're tempted to say something unkind, remember that your words can and should be helpful to others, not hurtful. God wants to use you to make this world a better place, and He will use the things that you say to help accomplish that goal . . . if you let Him.

Giving encouragement to others is
a most welcome gift, for the results of it
are lifted spirits, increased self-worth,
and a hopeful future.

Florence Littauer

We urgently need people who encourage
and inspire us to move toward God
and away from the world's enticing pleasures.

Jim Cymbala

TODAY'S BRIGHT IDEA

When talking to other people, ask yourself
this question: "How helpful can I be?"

PRAYER OF THE DAY

Dear Lord, I want my words to help
other people. Let me choose my words
carefully so that when I speak,
the world is a better place because of
the things I have said.
Amen

DAY 12

WHEN YOU'RE IN A HURRY

Wait for the Lord's help. Be strong
and brave and wait for the Lord's help.

Psalm 27:14 ICB

Sometimes, the hardest thing to do is to wait. This is especially true when we're in a hurry and when we want things to happen now, if not sooner! But God's plan does not always happen in the way that we would like or at the time of our own choosing. Still, God always knows best.

Sometimes, even though we may want something very badly, we must still be patient and wait for the right time to get it. And the right time, of course, is determined by God, not by us.

The busier we are, the easier it is to worry,
the greater the temptation to worry,
the greater the need to be alone with God.

Charles Stanley

Often our lives are strangled by things
that don't ultimately matter.

Grady Nutt

TODAY'S BRIGHT IDEA

Controlling yourself by slowing yourself down:
Sometimes, the best way to control yourself
is to slow yourself down. Then, you can think
about the things you're about to do before
you do them.

PRAYER OF THE DAY

Dear Lord, I want to be able to
control myself better and better
each day. Help me find better
ways to behave myself
that are pleasing to You.
Amen

DAY 13

MORE PATIENT EVERY DAY

A foolish person loses his temper.
But a wise person controls his anger.

Proverbs 29:11 ICB

D o you want to become a person who is perfectly patient? And would you like to become that person today? Sorry! You've got to be patient, even when it comes to becoming more patient!

It's impossible to grow up all at once. Instead, we must grow up a little each day. And that's the way it is with patience: we can become a little more patient each day, and we should try our best to do so. When we do, we grow up to become wise adults. And just think: we will have acquired all that wisdom one day at a time!

With each new dawn, life delivers
a package to your front door,
rings your doorbell, and runs.

Charles Swindoll

Every day we live is a priceless gift of God,
loaded with possibilities to learn
something new, to gain fresh insights.

Dale Evans Rogers

TODAY'S BRIGHT IDEA

Be patient with others and with yourself:
an important part of growing up is learning
to be patient with others and with yourself.
And one more thing: learn from everybody's
mistakes, especially your own.

PRAYER OF THE DAY

Dear Lord, let me become a little more grown up every day. Let me become the kind of person that You want me to be, Lord, and then let me keep growing up every day that I live.
Amen

DAY 14

WHEN THINGS GO WRONG

Be patient when trouble comes.
Pray at all times.
Romans 12:12 ICB

From time to time, all of us have to face troubles and disappointments.

When we do, God is always ready to protect us. Psalm 147 promises, "He heals the brokenhearted" (v. 3 NIV), but it doesn't say that He heals them instantly. Usually, it takes time for God to heal His children.

If you find yourself in any kind of trouble, pray about it and ask God for help. And then be patient. God will work things out, just as He has promised, but He will do it in His own time and according to His own plan.

Each problem is a God-appointed instructor.

Charles Swindoll

One sees great things from the valley,
only small things from the peak.

G. K. Chesterton

TODAY'S BRIGHT IDEA

You can make it right . . . if you think you
can! If you've made a mistake, apologize.
If you've broken something, fix it. If you've
hurt someone's feelings, apologize. If you
failed at something, try again. There is always
something you can do to make things better
. . . so do it!

PRAYER OF THE DAY

Dear Lord, sometimes life is so hard,
but with You, there is always hope.
Keep me mindful that there is nothing
that will happen today that You
and I can't handle together.
Amen

DAY 15

SPEAKING THE RIGHT WORDS AT THE RIGHT TIME

The right word spoken at the right time is as beautiful as gold apples in a silver bowl.

Proverbs 25:11 ICB

Sometimes, it's easier to say the wrong thing than it is to say the right thing—especially if we're in a hurry to blurt out the first words that come into our heads. But, if we are patient and if we choose our words carefully, we can help other people feel better, and that's exactly what God wants us to do.

The Book of Proverbs tells us that the right words, spoken at the right time, can be wonderful gifts to our families and to our friends. That's why we should think about the things that we say before we say them, not after. When we do, our words make the world a better place, and that's exactly what God wants!

Every word we speak, every action we take,
has an effect on the totality of humanity.
No one can escape that privilege—
or that responsibility.

Laurie Beth Jones

Like dynamite, God's power is only latent
power until it is released. You can release
God's dynamite power into people's lives
and the world through faith,
your words, and prayer.

Bill Bright

TODAY'S BRIGHT IDEA

To find golden words, use the Golden Rule:
when choosing the right words to say to
someone else, think about the words that you
would want to hear if you were standing in
their shoes.

PRAYER OF THE DAY

Dear Lord, if I choose my words carefully, I can make everybody happier, including myself. Today and every day, help me choose the words that You want me to speak so that I can make my corner of the world a better place to live.

Amen

DAY 16

IT'S UP TO YOU

We must not become tired of doing good.
We will receive our harvest of eternal life
at the right time. We must not give up!

Galatians 6:9 ICB

Nobody can be patient for you. You've got to be patient for yourself.

Certainly your parents can teach you about patience, but when it comes to controlling your temper, nobody can control it for you; you've got to control it yourself.

In the Book of Galatians, Paul writes, "We must not tire of doing good." And that's an important lesson: even when we're tired or frustrated, we must do our best to do the right thing.

So the next time you're tempted to lose your temper, stop for a moment and remember that when it comes to good deeds and good behavior, it's up to you.

Man's great danger is the combination
of his increased control over the elements
and his lack of control over himself.

Albert Schweitzer

Your thoughts are the determining factor
as to whose mold you are conformed to.
Control your thoughts and you control
the direction of your life.

Charles Stanley

TODAY'S BRIGHT IDEA

Don't try to blame other people for the
mistakes you make . . . When you point your
finger at someone else, the rest of your fingers
are pointing back at you!

PRAYER OF THE DAY

Dear Lord, there is a right way
and a wrong way to behave.
Let me remember that it's my job
to behave myself and to be the kind
of Christian that I know You want me
to be . . . today and always.
Amen

PATIENCE AT HOME

A foolish person loses his temper.
But a wise person controls his anger.

Proverbs 29:11 ICB

Sometimes, it's easiest to become angry with the people we love most. After all, we know that they'll still love us no matter how angry we become. But even though it's easy to become angry at home, it's usually wrong.

The next time you're tempted to become angry with a brother or a sister or a parent, remember that these are the people who love you more than anybody else! Then, calm down. Peace is always beautiful, especially when it's peace at your house.

The first essential for a happy home is love.
Billy Graham

Calm and peaceful, the home should be
the one place where people are certain
they will be welcomed, received,
protected, and loved.
Ed Young

TODAY'S BRIGHT IDEA

Speak respectfully to everybody, starting with
parents, grandparents, teachers, and other
adults . . . but don't stop there. Be respectful
of all people, including yourself!

PRAYER OF THE DAY

Dear Lord, make me respectful of
all people, and when I become angry
with my family and friends, let me be
quick to forgive and forget.
Let me be a patient, kind, loving
Christian today and always.
Amen

DAY 18

WORDS ARE
IMPORTANT

Pleasant words are like a honeycomb.
They make a person happy and healthy.

Proverbs 16:24 ICB

When we become angry, we may say things that are hurtful to other people. But when we strike out at others with the intention to hurt them, we are not doing God's will. God intends that His children treat others with patience, kindness, dignity, and respect. As Christians, we must do our best to obey our Creator.

Are you tempted to say an unkind word? Don't! Words are important, and once you say them, you can't call them back. But if you're wise, you won't need to!

Words. Do you fully understand their power?
Can any of us really grasp the mighty force
behind the things we say? Do we stop and
think before we speak, considering
the potency of the words we utter?

Joni Eareckson Tada

We give strength to our souls as we
train ourselves to speak words of
thankfulness and praise.

Annie Chapman

TODAY'S BRIGHT IDEA

Stop, think, then speak: If you want to make
your words useful instead of hurtful, don't
open your mouth until you've turned on your
brain and given it time to warm up.

PRAYER OF THE DAY

Dear Lord, make me a person of
patience and kindness. Make the things
that I say and do helpful to others,
so that through me,
they might see You.
Amen

DAY 19

IT STARTS ON
THE INSIDE

God's holy people must be patient.
They must obey God's commands
and keep their faith in Jesus.

Revelation 14:12 ICB

Where does patience start? It starts on the inside and works its way out. When our hearts are right with God, patience is a natural consequence of our love for Him.

Psalm 37:7 commands us to wait patiently for God, but, for most of us, waiting quietly for Him is difficult. Why? Because we are imperfect people who seek immediate answers to our problems. We don't like to wait for anybody or anything. But, God instructs us to be patient in all things, and that is as it should be. After all, think how patient God has been with us.

He doesn't need an abundance of words.
He doesn't need a dissertation
about your life. He just wants your attention.
He wants your heart.

Kathy Troccoli

Righteousness comes only from God.

Kay Arthur

TODAY'S BRIGHT IDEA

God and your parents have been patient with
you . . . now it's your turn to be patient with
others.

PRAYER OF THE DAY

Dear Lord, give me patience in matters
both great and small. You have been
patient with me, Lord; let me be loving,
patient, and kind to my family
and to my friends, today and always.
Amen

BEING PATIENT WITH PARENTS

Honor your father and your mother.

Exodus 20:25 ICB

Nobody's perfect, not even your parents. So the next time you're tempted to become angry with mom or dad for something they did or didn't do, stop and think about how much your parents do for you.

Sometimes, it's hard being a kid; that's for sure. But it can also be hard being a parent. Being a parent is a job with plenty of work to do, plenty of responsibilities to shoulder, and plenty of decisions to make. And if your parents make a bad decision every now and then, that's to be expected. So be patient with your parents . . . very patient. They've earned it.

Why is parental authority so vigorously supported throughout the Bible? By learning to yield to the loving authority of his parents, a child learns to submit to other forms of authority that will confront him later in life.

James Dobson

The child that never learns to obey his parents in the home will not obey God or man out of the home.

Susanna Wesley

TODAY'S BRIGHT IDEA

Calm down . . . sooner rather than later! If you're angry with your mom or your dad, don't blurt out something unkind. If you can't say anything nice, go to your room and don't come out until you can.

PRAYER OF THE DAY

Dear Lord, make me patient
and respectful toward my parents;
let me give them honor and love;
and let my behavior be pleasing
to them . . . and to You.
Amen

PEACE IS WONDERFUL

I leave you peace. My peace I give you.
I do not give it to you as the world does.
So don't let your hearts be troubled.

John 14:27 ICB

Patience and peace go together. And the beautiful words from John 14:27 remind us that Jesus offers us peace, not as the world gives, but as He alone gives. We, as believers, can accept His peace or ignore it. When we accept the peace of Jesus Christ into our hearts, our lives are changed forever, and we become more loving, patient Christians.

Christ's peace is offered freely; it has already been paid for; it is ours for the asking. So let us ask . . . and then share.

Peace is better than a fortune.

St. Francis of Sales

God is in control of history; it's His story.
Doesn't that give you a great peace—
especially when world events seem so
tumultuous and insane?

Kay Arthur

TODAY'S BRIGHT IDEA

Count to ten . . . but don't stop there! If
you're angry with someone, don't say the first
thing that comes to your mind. Instead, catch
your breath and start counting until you are
once again in control of your temper. If you
get to a million and you're still counting, go to
bed! You'll feel better in the morning.

PRAYER OF THE DAY

Dear Lord, help me to accept
Your peace and then to share it
with others, today and forever.
Amen

DAY 22

BEING A PATIENT FRIEND

A friend loves you all the time.

Proverbs 17:17 ICB

Having friends requires patience. From time to time, even our most considerate friends may do things that make us angry. Why? Because they are not perfect. Neither, of course, are we.

Today and every day, let us be understanding and patient with our friends. If we forgive them when they make mistakes, then perhaps they will forgive us when we make mistakes. And then, because we are patient and forgiving with each other, we will build friendships that will last.

Just thinking about a friend makes you want to do a happy dance, because a friend is someone who loves you in spite of your faults.

Charles Schulz

Life is a chronicle of friendship.
Friends create the world anew each day.
Without their loving care, courage would not suffice to keep hearts strong for life.

Helen Keller

TODAY'S BRIGHT IDEA

If you're having trouble forgiving someone else . . . think how many times other people have forgiven you!

PRAYER OF THE DAY

Dear Lord, let me be patient
and understanding toward my friends.
Lord, help me to remember that we
all make mistakes and to forgive them,
like You have forgiven me.
Amen

DAY 23

WHAT THE BIBLE SAYS

Your word is like a lamp for my feet
and a light for my way.

Psalm 119:105 ICB

Are you having trouble with your temper, or with anything else for that matter? The answer to your problems can be found in God's Holy Word: the Bible.

The Bible is God's instruction book for living. If you learn what the Bible says, and if you follow its instructions, you will be blessed now and forever. So get to know your Bible; it's never too soon to become an expert on God's Word.

I believe the Bible is the best gift
God has given to man.

Abraham Lincoln

God spoke in His word.
He is still speaking in it and through it.
We, in turn, must get to know God.

S. D. Gordon

TODAY'S BRIGHT IDEA

Take care of your Bible! It's the most
important book you own . . . by far!

PRAYER OF THE DAY

Dear Lord, You have given me
a marvelous gift: the Holy Bible.
Let me read it and understand
it and believe it and follow the
commandments that I find there—
every day that I live.
Amen

IT'S BETTER TO BE PATIENT

Patience is better than strength.

Proverbs 16:32 ICB

In the Book of Proverbs, we are told that patience is a very good thing. But for most of us, patience can also be a very hard thing. After all, we have many things that we want, and we want them NOW! But the Bible tells us that we must learn to wait patiently for the things that God has in store for us.

Are you having trouble being patient? If so, remember that patience takes practice, and lots of it, so keep trying. And if you make a mistake, don't be too upset. After all, if you're going to be a really patient person, you shouldn't just be patient with others; you should also be patient with yourself.

God is never in a hurry.
Oswald Chambers

God is more patient with us than
we are with ourselves.
Max Lucado

TODAY'S BRIGHT IDEA

Take a deep breath, a very deep breath: if
you think you're about to say or do something
you'll regret later, slow down and take a deep
breath or two deep breaths or ten, or . . .
well, you get the point.

PRAYER OF THE DAY

Dear Lord, the Bible tells me that
it's better to be patient than impulsive.
Help me to slow myself down
so I can make better decisions
today and every day.
Amen

DAY 25

ALWAYS GROWING UP

But grow in the special favor and knowledge
of our Lord and Savior Jesus Christ.
To him be all glory and honor,
both now and forevermore. Amen.

2 Peter 3:18 NLT

When do we stop growing up? Hopefully never! If we keep studying God's Word, and if we obey His commandments, we will never be "fully grown" Christians. We will always be growing.

God intends that we continue growing in the love and knowledge of Christ. And when we do so, we become more patient, more loving, more understanding, and more Christ-like. And we keep growing and growing . . . and growing!

Trying to grow up hurts. You make mistakes.
You try to learn from them, and when you
don't, it hurts even more.

Aretha Franklin

To be successful, one must grow to the point
where he completely forgets himself;
that is, loses himself in a great cause.

Booker T. Washington

TODAY'S BRIGHT IDEA

Read the Bible? Yes! Try to read the Bible
with your parents every day. If they forget,
remind them!

PRAYER OF THE DAY

Dear Lord, let me keep learning about
Your love and Your Son as long as
I live. Make me a better person today
than I was yesterday, but not as good
a person as I can become tomorrow
if I continue to trust in You.
Amen

BEING PATIENT WITH EVERYBODY

I tell you the truth, anything you did for even the least of my people here, you also did for me.

Matthew 25:40 NCV

The Bible tells us that we should be patient with everybody, not just with parents, teachers, and friends. In the eyes of God, all people are very important, so we should treat them that way.

Of course it's easy to be nice to the people whom we want to impress, but what about everybody else? Jesus gave us clear instructions: He said that when we do a good deed for someone less fortunate than we are, we have also done a good deed for our Savior. And as Christians, that's exactly what we are supposed to do!

Make it a rule, and pray to God to help you
to keep it, never, if possible, to lie down
at night without being able to say:
"I have made one human being at least
a little wiser, or a little happier,
or at least a little better this day."

Charles Kingsley

No one stands taller in the climb
to success than when he bends over
to help up someone else.

John Maxwell

TODAY'S BRIGHT IDEA

Everybody is a VIP: VIP means "Very
Important Person." To God, everybody is a
VIP, and we should treat every person with
dignity, patience, and respect.

PRAYER OF THE DAY

Dear Lord, help me to be patient
with everyone I meet. Help me to be
respectful of all people, and help me
to say kind words and do good deeds,
today and every day.

Amen

DAY 27

STOP AND THINK

A wise person's mind tells him what to say.

Proverbs 16:23 ICB

When we lose control of our emotions, we do things that we shouldn't do. Sometimes, we throw tantrums. How silly! Other times we pout or whine. Too bad!

The Bible tells us that it is foolish to become angry and that it is wise to remain calm. That's why we should learn to slow down and to think about things before we do them.

Do you want to make life better for yourself and for your family? Then be patient and think things through. Stop and think before you do things, not after. It's the wise thing to do.

Patience is the companion of wisdom.
St. Augustine

Patient waiting is often the highest way of doing God's will.
St. Francis de Sales

TODAY'S BRIGHT IDEA

Tantrums? No way! If you think you might lose your temper, stop and catch your breath, and walk away if you must. It's better to walk away than it is to let your temper control you.

PRAYER OF THE DAY

Dear Lord, I can be so impatient,
and I can become so angry.
Calm me down, Lord, and make me
a patient, forgiving Christian,
today and every day of my life.
Amen

DAY 28

AVOIDING QUARRELS

Foolish people are always getting into
quarrels, but avoiding quarrels
will bring you honor.

Proverbs 20:3 ICB

In Proverbs, King Solomon gave us wonderful advice for living wisely. Solomon warned that impatience and anger lead only to trouble. And he was right!

The next time you're tempted to say an unkind word or to start an argument, remember Solomon. He was one of the wisest men who ever lived, and he knew that it's always better to be patient. So remain calm, and remember that patience is best. After all, if it's good enough for a wise man like Solomon, it should be good enough for you, too.

Argument is the worst sort of conversation.
Jonathan Swift

Some fights are lost even though we win.
A bulldog can whip a skunk,
but it just isn't worth it.
Vance Havner

TODAY'S BRIGHT IDEA

Tempted to fight? Walk away. The best fights
are those that never happen.

PRAYER OF THE DAY

Dear Lord, when I become angry,
help me to remember that You offer
me peace. Let me turn to You for
wisdom, for patience, and for
the peace that only You can give.
Amen

IF YOU NEED HELP, ASK GOD!

We pray that the Lord will lead your hearts
into God's love and Christ's patience.

2 Thessalonians 3:5 ICB

Do you need help in becoming a more patient person? If so, ask God; He's always ready, willing, and able to help. In fact, the Bible promises that when we sincerely seek God's help, He will give us the things we need.

So, if you want to become a better person, bow your head and start praying about it. And then rest assured that with God's help, you can change for the better . . . and you will!

God makes prayer as easy as possible for us.
He's completely approachable and available,
and He'll never mock or upbraid us for
bringing our needs before Him.

Shirley Dobson

Don't be afraid to ask your heavenly Father
for anything you need. Indeed, nothing is
too small for God's attention
or too great for his power.

Dennis Swanberg

TODAY'S BRIGHT IDEA

Don't be too hard on yourself: you don't have
to be perfect to be wonderful. God loves you
. . . and you should too.

PRAYER OF THE DAY

Dear Lord, I have so much to learn
and so many ways to improve myself,
but You love me just as I am.
Thank You for Your love and for
Your Son. And, help me to
become the person that You
want me to become.
Amen

DAY 30

WITH LOVE IN YOUR HEART

So these three things continue forever:
faith, hope, and love.
And the greatest of these is love.

1 Corinthians 13:13 ICB

The words of 1 Corinthians 13:13 remind us that love is God's commandment: "But now abide faith, hope, love, these three; but the greatest of these is love" (NASB). Faith is important, of course. So is hope. But, love is more important still.

Christ loved us first, and, as Christians, we are called upon to return His love by sharing it. Today, let's share Christ's love with our families and friends. When we do, we'll discover that a loving heart is also a patient heart. And, we'll discover that the more we love, the more patient we become.

In the presence of love, miracles happen.

Robert Schuller

To show great love for God and our neighbor,
we need not do great things. It is how much
love we put in the doing that makes
our offering something beautiful for God.

Mother Teresa

TODAY'S BRIGHT IDEA

Pray for a heart that is loving and patient,
and remember that God answers prayer!

PRAYER OF THE DAY

Dear Lord, give me a heart
that is filled with love, patience, and
concern for others. Slow me down
and calm me down so that I can see
the needs of other people.
And then, give me a loving heart
so that I will do something about
the needs that I see.
Amen

BIBLE VERSES
TO MEMORIZE

Be gentle to all, able to teach, patient.

2 Timothy 2:24 NKJV

Honor your father and your mother.

Exodus 20:12 ICB

Foolish people are always
getting into quarrels, but avoiding
quarrels will bring you honor.

Proverbs 20:3 ICB

Where the Spirit of the Lord is, there is freedom.

2 Corinthians 3:17 NIV

The right word spoken
at the right time is as beautiful
as gold apples in a silver bowl.

Proverbs 25:11 ICB

Patience is better than pride.

Ecclesiastes 7:8 NLT

A friend loves you all the time.

Proverbs 17:17 ICB

Show respect for all people.
Love the brothers and sisters
of God's family.

1 Peter 2:17 ICB

Be still before the Lord and wait patiently for Him.

Psalm 37:7 NIV

Do not worry about anything.
But pray and ask God
for everything you need.

Philippians 4:6 ICB

The Lord is the strength of my life.

Psalm 27:1 KJV

But if we look forward to something
we don't have yet, we must wait
patiently and confidently.

Romans 8:25 NLT

Do for other people the same things you want them to do for you.

Matthew 7:12 ICB

Live peaceful
and quiet lives in all
godliness and holiness.

1 Timothy 2:2 NIV

Patience is better than strength.

Proverbs 16:32 ICB

I leave you peace. My peace I give you.
I do not give it to you
as the world does.
So don't let your hearts be troubled.

John 14:27 ICB

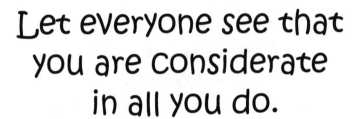

Let everyone see that you are considerate in all you do.

Philippians 4:5 NLT

Blessed are the peacemakers,
because they
will be called sons of God.

Matthew 5:9 HCSB

Don't ever stop being kind
and truthful.
Let kindness and truth
show in all you do.

Proverbs 3:3 ICB

Lead a quiet
and peaceable life
in all godliness and
honesty.

1 Timothy 2:2 KJV

You shall not steal, nor deal falsely, nor lie to one another.

Leviticus 19:11 NASB

I have given you
an example to follow.
Do as I have done to you.

John 13:15 NLT

Always be humble and gentle.
Be patient and accept each other with love.

Ephesians 4:2 ICB

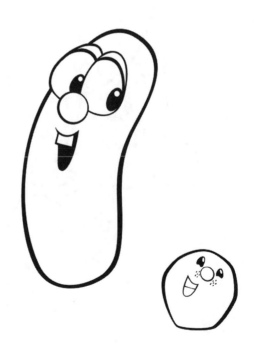